BE A MERMAID

& be independent, be powerful, be free

BE A MERMAID

& be independent, be powerful, be free

SARAH FORD

ILLUSTRATED BY
ANITA MANGAN

spruce

FOR DEBBIE

NOTES

Read this book to reach your full potential.

Contains a healthy dose of equality.

Rated GP... for girl power.

You go, girl.

Be a mermaid. Why? Because she is the original independent woman: fierce, pleasure-seeking and a true force of nature.

Happy in the sea or on land, Mermaid is a passionate lover of life. She will fight for her rights and for what she believes in, and her strong moral code and love of the planet guide all her decisions. Mermaid believes in herself and won't let anything stand in her way. She chooses her friends wisely and is loyal to the end.

Mermaid is not afraid of her emotions, but she is also not ruled by them. Her true spirit and headstrong nature make her quite a force to be reckoned with... better to have her as a friend than as an enemy. Seductive and charming, Mermaid is not known as the goddess of the sea for nothing, and she loves a good debate and will speak her mind with conviction in order to further a good cause. She believes that all men, women and creatures are created equal and that mutual respect will lead to a happy and fulfilled life.

10 SIGNS YOU'RE A MERMAID

- You make every moment count, and seize every opportunity that comes your way.

- You are always true to yourself.

- You desire coast and sea over town and city.

- Beachcombing is your thing – you're obsessed with shells and sea glass (who needs diamonds)?

- You fear the shallows more than the depths.

- You love riding on the crest of waves – the bigger, the better.

- You have a love of all things bright.

- You are happy swimming with sharks.

- You often dream of water, the sea, waterfalls, streams and lakes.

- Your dream job involves caring for the environment, both above and under the water.

Mermaid liked to be
referred to as Ms.

Mermaid was eating dessert for dinner.

Mermaid dived in
head-first and made
a big splash.

Mermaid made sure
everyone was paid
the same.

Mermaid was not
scared to make the
first move.

Mermaid thought there wasn't anything she couldn't do, apart from paint her toenails.

Mermaid had no
need to compare
herself to others.

Mermaid carried
the universe close
to her heart.

Mermaid was
unapologetic.

Mermaid was very
happy eating alone
in restaurants.

Mermaid thought
there was nothing to
fear but fear itself.

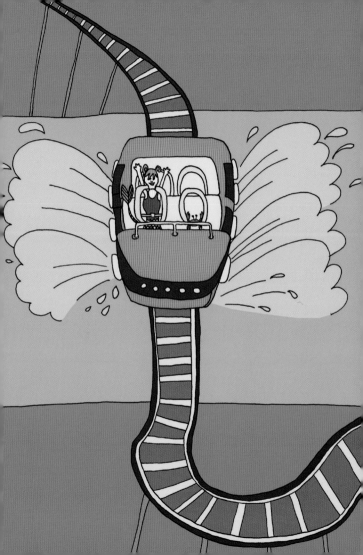

Mermaid was not about
to wait in for the phone
to ring.

While diving for pearls, Mermaid also found some beautiful sea glass.

Mermaid thought
Disney needed to
rewrite the script.

Mermaid thought
bare-faced cheeks
and made-up
cheeks were
equally beautiful.

The only time Mermaid
wished she could wear
high heels was at concerts.

Mermaid was giving
needy people the boot.

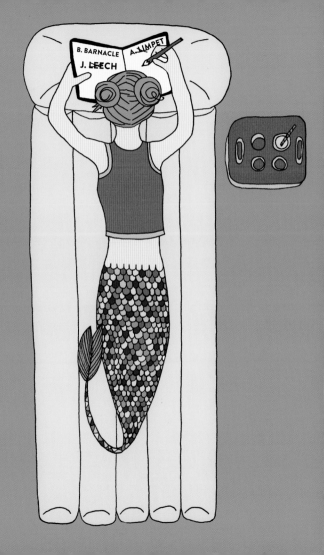

They might have been hit
by the ugly stick but they
were Mermaid's most
interesting friends.

Mermaid was
undaunted by her
new environment.

Mermaid was not
going to waste time
sitting on a rock.

Mermaid's clothes
were an extension of
her personality.

EQUAL
RIGHTS
FOR ALL
FISH

Mermaid did not make
snap judgments.

Mermaid was taking a mental health holiday.

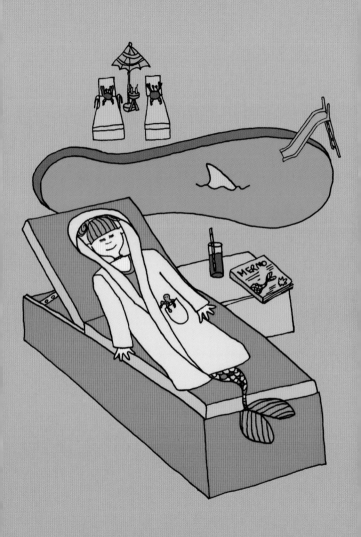

Mermaid was going
to make sure that she
was heard.

Mermaid only
ever dressed to
impress herself.

Mermaid was
thinking big.

Cakey Cakey Bakery

Mermaid knew that
her tribe had her back.

Mermaid always
remembered to
call home.

Mermaid was looking forward to growing older disgracefully.

Mermaid thought
that there was no
such thing as guilty
pleasures, there were
just pleasures.

Mermaid had a lot of
blessings to count.

If all else failed,
Mermaid went with
her intuition.

Mermaid had found
a sense of balance.

Mermaid was enjoying
the sound of silence.

Optimistic people
attract good things,
thought Mermaid.

For Mermaid, it was
water off a duck's back.

Mermaid liked the
security of home.

Mermaid was not afraid
to make waves.

There were plenty
of fish in the sea,
and then there
was Mermaid.

Mermaid always
bought her own drinks.

Mermaid was seeking
the right type of
attention.

Mermaid was leader
of the litter pick.

Mermaid loved
fiercely.

Mermaid was following
her own path. Now be
like Mermaid, and do
the same.

An Hachette UK Company
www.hachette.co.uk

First published in Great Britain in
2018 by Spruce, a division of
Octopus Publishing Group Ltd
Carmelite House
50 Victoria Embankment
London EC4Y 0DZ
www.octopusbooks.co.uk

Distributed in the US by
Hachette Book Group
1290 Avenue of the Americas
4th and 5th Floors
New York, NY 10104

Distributed in Canada by
Canadian Manda Group
664 Annette St.
Toronto, Ontario, Canada M6S 2C8

ISBN 978-1-84601-563-2

A CIP catalogue record for this
book is available from the British
Library.

Printed and bound in China

10 9 8 7 6 5 4 3 2 1

Commissioning Editor
Sarah Ford

Assistant Editor
Ellie Corbett

Designer and Illustrator
Anita Mangan

Senior Designer
Jaz Bahra

Production Controller
Sarah Kulasek-Boyd